SPIRITS

*For Michael,
looking forward to more
seafood, poetry
and good fellowship.
Cheers,*

Dan Epstein

May, 1992

Books by Daniel Mark Epstein

Poems

NO VACANCIES IN HELL
THE FOLLIES
YOUNG MEN'S GOLD
THE BOOK OF FORTUNE

Prose

STAR OF WONDER
THE HEATH GUIDE TO POETRY
THE HEATH GUIDE TO LITERATURE

Plays

JENNY AND THE PHOENIX
THE MIDNIGHT VISITOR

POEMS BY DANIEL MARK EPSTEIN

SPIRITS

THE OVERLOOK PRESS/WOODSTOCK, NEW YORK

FOR DAVID BERGMAN

Some of these poems have appeared in the
following magazines, to whose editors grate-
ful acknowledgment is made: *America, The
American Scholar, Fiction International, Harvard
Magazine, The Kenyon Review, Michigan
Quarterly Review, The New Criterion, The
Paris Review, Poetry Miscellany, Prairie
Schooner, The Smith, The Virginia Quarterly
Review* and *The Washingtonian*. "Homage To
Mallarmé" was inspired by the prose poems
"Plainte d'automne," "Frisson d'hiver," and
"Le nénuphar blanc." I would like to thank
Richard Howard and Robert Peters for their
helpful suggestions. I would also like to thank
the John Simon Guggenheim Foundation for
a fellowship that assisted me in completing
this book.

First published in 1987 by
The Overlook Press
Lewis Hollow Road
Woodstock, New York 12498

Library of Congress Cataloging-in-Publication Data

Epstein, Daniel Mark.
  Spirits.

  I. Title.
PS3555.P65S65 1987   811'.54   86-31214
ISBN 0-87951-273-3 (cloth)
ISBN 0-87951-274-1 (paper)

CONTENTS

CYGNUS MUSICUS

Note the scale of tones that flies from a brass bugle
and, trusting that Nature creates nothing in vain,
compare the horn's shape to the windpipe of a swan,
that snaky tube of bony rings. You see
the bird's instrument is altogether equal
to playing the music praised in antiquity:
those plaintive strains, a cello-like requiem
murmuring through the reeds its prophetic sigh
as death waves the swan toward asylum where
no one may hear him sing, no other bird
break up the sacrament of his dying hymn.

Also in the windless glow of a sea-beach
they sing before sunrise, says Oppian.
Pythagoras was so moved he began to teach
that the poet's soul in death becomes a swan
so his divine harmony will not be lost.
One night before Plato came to Socrates
the sage dreamed a swan hid in his breast;
and hours from execution the swan sounded
to him like a joyous prophecy of the Good
waiting for us there in the next kingdom,
and not some hyperbole of bestial dread.

Now it seems the swan's melodic gift is fading
   or one must be dead to hear it. I have stood
long hours by lakes and estuarine rivers
   and recall only a stridulous braying, though none
of my subjects was ever summoned by death
   the singing master. I will go on straining
my ears in the twilight between hope and dread
   I shall catch that mythic descant of the swan,
out of my senses at last to hear the singing,
   like a father who hears the voice of his lost son,
that supreme fantasia, the soul's returning.

THE BRIDE'S PROFILE

She cannot see her profile in the mirror,
    a blessing, the painter would insist,
the mystic Heinrich Bebie, circa 1850,
    easel propped in the entry of the bride's
chamber, chimes before the wedding. O
    not that she lacks charm! The waterfall
of veils discloses nape and arm and breast
    to overwhelm the bridegroom's fantasy.

A jewel box agape on the dresser top
    has yielded up the pearls of her trousseau.
Between the leaning bride and her mirror image,
    a boat-shaped urn of gold glows—at the bow
a sculpted cherub, at the stern, for grip,
    a tiny maid that might pass for a boy.
The sylph's head is sainted by the halo
    of the mirrored bride's camellia corsage.

Better, Bebie muses, she cannot see
    the mirror at this moment. Although
reflections are mere accidents of light,
    of life confronting life momentarily:
a girl stunned by her beauty suddenly,
    or woman by its loss, a meditative willow
drawn into a glassy stream that carries away
    its picture invisibly to be whirled and broken

among rocks and rapids, distilled in crystal spray—
    although no reflection is to be trusted
it is better she cannot see herself in profile.
    Quite enough that I should stand and witness
the bride's profile under the chaplet of pinks,
    her milky brow, the maiden tenderness
harden in the mirror. The cruel twin yoked
    with the oblivious bride, gazing parallel,

hawk-nosed, hawk-eyed, lips galled to a line,
    glares at the bride's dream that was her doom
and curses with wedged eye a bearded man
    who haunts the faded doorway of the mirror.
When I am dead, thinks Bebie, some will wonder
    who was that weary spectre in the doorway,
lingering, too old to be the groom.
    It is the man who will give the bride away.

CHAMPAGNE

All the angels that might fit
on the head of a pin,
every spirit with its petty sin
must pass through here
on the way to bliss.

They appear out of nowhere
in silver chains
rising through the clear crucible,
and scatter in the gold
to dance for us,

then at the crystal heights
burst into chorus.

RAPHAEL

1

The gallery light left something to be desired.
Electric ghosts in clouds and streaks
told their moral on the bulletproof glass:
the soul will make a mirror of any window.
I shifted. It made no difference at all.
From where I looked into the constant space
of your self-portrait, my own face
shot back at me from your burnished eye
like the floating image on a gypsy's ball.

Poor Narcissus. If he could have seen
your clear eyes spending light
as if the generous stream where lovers bend
to drink each other's images
ran to and from your vision's hidden spring;
had Narcissus seen such eyes within
the silver of the pool, he might have known
a luckier myth and lived it, loving
a face far more beautiful than his own.

Just whisper, and I will sound an echo
in the bowl of viridian hills around Urbino,
in the high-walled gunmetal streets of America.
Come live in these matchstick verses,
and leave the frail galleries of the world
where beauty wore out its welcome long ago.
One critic took an axe to the Pietà,
moved by pity to crush the Saviour's skull.
The world is a perilous museum now.

Your work survived a trial of centuries,
fire, flood and war. "Lo Spasimo,"
the Bearing of the Cross, shipwrecked en route
to the monks of Oliveto, rode the cold
waves to the port of Genoa unscathed.
When Rome was sacked four hundred years ago
French merchants tried to burn your tapestries,
char the silk and wool threads from the gold.
Your living figures blew their torches out.

Now a mock sun threatens every city
and there's scant breath left in humanity
to blow it out. Your pictures tremble on the wall
so we can hardly see them through the glass.
Man is in love with an image of himself
that has nothing to do with beauty.
It is a mask of terror, a hunchbacked elf
hailing the Last Judgment with bitter glee.
Whisper, and make our hearts your gallery.

2

Beryl blue, the Umbrian ravine
where an old man lived in solitude,
Father Bernardo, joyful anchorite.
Barren of all but faith, he claimed two daughters:
one the oak tree shading his frail hut,
and one a singing child of the vine dressers,
Mary, who brought his dole of bread and wine.
Two daughters, one silver-tongued, one mute.

December brought a shrill and barbarous gale
that furrowed Heaven's front and swelled the cheeks
of thunderheads that rioted over the hill,
sweeping deep-rooted pines from valley glades.
After the wind and rain, what little stood
tumbled under the stampede of a flood.
When clouds parted at last for the ruffled sun,
Mary went to see where Bernardo had gone

and learned how the silent daughter had saved him.
When freshets lashed his windowsill
he shinnied up a drain to the bark shingle.
When white waves came lapping at the eaves
he looked to the starless Heaven; whereupon
oak branches bowed low, beckoning him to climb
into their arms. Safe there in the crown
he prayed for his other daughter to help him down

and home to warm his bones and feed him bread,
for the storm had almost made an end of him.
How could he repay them? Prayer was all he had.
Bernardo called upon Heaven to bless
his daughters, the silver-tongued and the speechless,
praying Time would remember them together.
Time takes the pilgrim where he aims his hymn.
Climbing the golden verses ladderwise

Bernardo views the future: Mary wed,
the bloom-cheeked mother of two beaming sons.
The oak tree, felled, makes staves for a wine cask.
Mary rocks in the arbor, child at breast,
her tunic viridian, skirts blue berylline.
The toddler binds a cross of apple wood.
Out of a shadow strays a strange young man
rubbing his eyes as if this were a dream. It is

a dream, but what he makes of it proves real
beyond ages of human questioning.
He crayons on cracked staves of the wine cask
a breathing horizon of ripe womanhood,
circle of red-sleeved arms, head bowed to love
the pearl of a boy. O static ecstasy!
A gold-edged halo hums, lights from above
this pearl within the pearl, his grey-winged eye.

3

Even in death is no escaping
the broad joke of mortality.
Ambitious antiquarians
in 1833

had a skull they thought was yours
and nothing else would do
but dig up the floor of the Pantheon
trying to find you,

make sure you were all there,
make sure the casket was full.
They found your little skeleton
and, *mirabile dictu,* the skull!

Man's name is carved in his skull,
omo, a man, the same,
round eyes either side of the nose.
Death knows only one name.

King and Pope were summoned
to thank the Lord it was you.
Hurrah! said the crowd in Rome.
Hurrah for the glass case too

where your skeleton dangled before
you were laid in the marble tomb
to the tune of a hidden choir,
and everybody went home.

Nature feared to be conquered
while you lived. After you died
Nature feared for her life,
as if people and countryside

would fade with your vision.
The sun might sicken with grief,
flowers retire to the underworld,
the forest fall with the leaf.

The bright oculus winks above
Raphael's Pantheon tomb.
I would like to rest here with him
but there's no more dying room

on earth and little time
till Nature closes her doors
on the last of us. I will look
for my grave among the stars.

THE CARPENTER

Old enough to know her father's need
for sleep, she would not wake him with her cry.
Through quartered window glass the cold
rides on the moonlight flooding her room,
casting a shadow cross on the bare wall.
She would not cry although the light seems cruel

as winter, cutting through the quilts and sheet,
tightens its grip on her legs. The pain there
thrives on, though raised in the dull heat
of summer when fever with a brutal hand
yanked the legs from under her, folding them
back to kneel as if she must pray forever.

But something stirs her father. And he turns
in his own pain, wakeful, knowing her awake,
leaves his bed and climbs the narrow stair;
rising toward the moon in the window beside her,
he sees her speechless eyes and smooths her hair.
He pulls a chair up to the glass that shines

in its beveled skin of ice. A single fingernail
rough work has left intact, becomes his tool
scratching on one quarter of the pane: a flower.
His daughter smiles to see it bloom in silver
on the moonlit wall, the first of a full garden
where two lovers are walking hand in hand.

It has been years since he has known /
this freedom of making, since necessity
bartered plane and chisel for his pen.
He moves on to the second pane, a woman rocking
a child, its curled hand reaching for her lips,
her hair bound in a low hive but for a strand.

His daughter's eyes are moonwide now, yet calm,
eager for the next image. His cold hand
etches on the third pane a fine rose window
and altar rail where a young woman is kneeling,
her dress and petticoats ruffled like a peony,
under the priest's blessing, her first communion.

Smiling, she nods. One pane is frosted blind.
He cannot think to move his hand, it moves
as her eyes close, rescued from this vision:
he draws a hill and road that winds behind
where men and women vanish two by two,
climbing in slow procession, following, what?

The sudden heat of breath and hands has made
a rainstorm on the landscape—his work is done.
He kisses her asleep. On the stray fringe
of frozen light from the golden mural he gropes
his way downstairs, thanking the full moon,
knowing the sun will never be so kind.

THINKING OF THOMAS MOORE

A book that I knew only by the cover,
climbed to a high shelf on a crumbling ramp
years ago, the relic of an old affair.
I took it down, hoping to find out
how one famous bard ran out of fame
and why he had come to haunt me suddenly.
I cracked the book. There was his Irish pout
engraved on the flyleaf, a spiteful genie
whose gratitude grew bitter in the lamp.

The curl of his lip, the eye's tenacity,
show us Tom Moore was not prepared to die,
at least not in print. A preface tells
his life. Born in Dublin, a grocer's son,
he studied with the tutor of Sheridan,
at fourteen enrolled at Trinity,
wrote the sensational "Odes of Anacreon"
that made him a star before the age of twenty.
Small of stature, "though in wit a man,"

he never grew up. But he sold more
poems than anyone but Byron who
called them "leadless pistols" in a satire.
Moore sent the modern Juvenal a challenge
then recalled it. They became fast friends.
When Byron died he left Moore as legacy
his *Memoirs* to transmute to pounds
in the crucible of public curiosity.
Tom committed them to a gentler fire.

London was shocked by his arrogance,
lack of gratitude or its excess, met
by heroic friendship or its opposite.
For scandal dines as heartily on silence
as on the juiciest gossip where
the subject is a free beauty or handsome poet.
The top blew off the kettle of conjecture.
His *Memoirs* might have served Byron's defense;
the fire branded him as a demon, sure.

But Byron has all the world to tell his story.
Moore has, at the moment, only me.
What about his poems, are there any
lost treasures under the waterfall
of foxed and fading pages, a fire opal
shaken from the crown of a classic beauty,
or merry trinket kicked from a dancer's ankle,
that rolled away flashing out of the world's sight?
I turn the pages out of a sense of duty.

There are the Irish melodies sung in the twilight
of parlors by deep-bosomed ladies and old men.
There are the chiseled "Odes of Anacreon"
in praise of deep drinking and shallow passion.
And page after page, until my eyes are sore,
love poems, love poems by Thomas Moore.
You'd think that little else was worth his time,
or worse, that there was nothing easier
than falling in love and then making it rhyme.

Whom did you love, Tom? What maid or whore
escaped your manicured verses? There's no sign
of struggle, not a curl or petticoat out of place,
nor desire that puts conscience on the rack.
Your ladies flirt and sigh. They don't talk back.
Oh world of harps and blushes, plumes and lace,
you remember the name of love but not the face.
What did you feel when the last one slammed the door
and how could you tell her from the one before?

Meanwhile a strong wind has attacked the casement
in Tom's defense, breaking up my irreverent
thoughts with louder thoughts that sound like wind
holding forth in the chimney, shaking the door
and drumming up the thunder for a storm.
Wind like thoughts, then wind in human form.
It is the furious ghost of Thomas Moore
rather dignified by death, or by the lightning.
"Who are you to disturb me in oblivion?"

"It's quiet here but I've gotten used to it
now that my friends are dead and I've stopped waiting
to be rediscovered. There's a worse thing
than being forgotten: false laurel, early fame
borrowed from an ancient poet's name.
I paid for that. And I paid for my height
in love affairs that never made a rhyme,
their pain was so much greater than my art.
Honor this pure silence, and mind your own heart."

THE DATE

Just as you were about to step out
in your sleek, black-sequined dress
fresh from the second-hand store, veteran chic
as only a fifty-year-old dress knows how to be—

just as you pulled the shades down by the ring
and shut the door, as you were walking
toward night and the rest of your life,
a lover, a quiet place where you might find one—

just as you stopped for the passing car
that braked so the boys could whistle as
you kicked back your leg, looked over your shoulder
to check if the stocking seam had run askew—

just as you passed outside the bar I saw you
as you saw yourself in the turtle-shell compact,
making sure it was the same you as left home—
just then you thought of my words, felt warm inside—

and now you must stay with me forever.

LATENESS

Because the past cannot bear to part with her
the present suffers. So we wait
in a lobby under the eyes of chandeliers,
in train stations, on a street corner,
and at midnight in the graveyard with a spirit
who waited in this world and waits in the next,

for her October hair and bright May skin
have taken since the beginning of earthly time
and will take forever. Time goes with her;
wherever she stops the moments turn and spin.
Little minutes are doves eating out of her hand—
but when the hours call she does not answer.

Because her worth is beyond question or value,
kings have died for her and worlds collided,
skies caved in and hills leapt in the blue.
Her touch can melt the icecaps, make
buttercups flash in the desert, and wild daisies.
Poets have climbed to Heaven, singing her praises.

It isn't for spite she keeps you waiting there
at the small end of night's telescope. No,
it's not to belittle you with your bruised corsage
and trail of crushed cigarettes, left behind,
your shadow of beard, the useless theater tickets.
You are probably the farthest thing from her mind.

Maybe a street singer took her by surprise, or
the pattern of a scarf, scarlet and pearl-grey
made her pause and muse in the window, then
the moon would not let her go until it passed.
Maybe later in the street, admiring children
circled her on skates and led her away

laughing, into a wide park where it seems
her gentle protests failed as she tried on
their silver wheels and showed them whirling figures
they had seen before only in dreams.
Because of this, and the endless flattery of twilight,
the gay breeze beneath the sad story of each star,

she must honor the times that make her beautiful.
And the wonder is not that she is late tonight
but that anyone has ever seen her at all.

THE GLASS

Arc of flying horses, lily fan,
earth-rooted seeds that flower in the brain,
and now this woman
with all the tricks of nature to multiply
leaf upon leaf and heartbeat upon beat,
has come to live in my mind, as if
the world were not wide enough to hold her beauty.

I see her every hour of the day.
Nights are not long enough, nor the halls
of dreams where we pass on the way
to the radiant memory of passing.
Darkness is not enough, the single gift
the underworld provides us while we live,
to serve as a background for fantasy.

Restless with nights and dreams
she has to stand
up white as a diamond lightning struck
in broad daylight, between me and the world.
When she walks into the room something must break,
mind's image meets her coming with such force.
My glass is shattered and I cannot speak.

PAS DE DEUX

Plucked from the night above that tivoli
    of amber strung zigzag along the shore
I feel like I have been picked up and thrown
    from blizzard to the tropics, door to door.
The wall of heat; palm trees in sulphur light,
    my name on a sign held by a stranger-host
who smiles like he has known me all my life;
    two ward-heelers, three-odd journalists,

briefcase, baggage, my flight-stunned guitar
    crowd a limousine to the Grand Hotel
where the night clerk begs my signature
    in trade for a folded note. My gilded key
rings on marble as I read her name,
    phone numbers: "Welcome. Call if you have time."
Faster than thought the chandelier cascades
    and columns sway, my footmen turn to mice,

the lobby spins, a giant clockface flies
    cartoonlike behind the night clerk's back.
Faster than light, time hurls me into the dark
    room in Bristol ten years ago, and
Botticelli's cherub, all lips and eyes
    above and imponderable roundnesses below,
our bed under skylight next to the window
    sailing to ecstasy on a surge of stars.

Strangers, two embraced until one cried
 we knew each other better than ourselves,
the lover's dream, or lie that has come true,
 the touchstone: such a brilliance I have tried
to measure by it every new caress,
 the cataclysms of my mind and blood,
judge joy and sorrow by that vividness
 which still assuages pain, humbles delight.

Ten years ago I left a girl in Bristol
 wondering would I ever see her again,
thought best to forget her, and could not.
 The girl became a woman whose beauty grew
fantastic as hope of finding her ran out
 and passing time said this is just desire's
handiwork, vain Galatea, unanswered prayer.
 Maybe this prodigy exists nowhere.

But I am to meet a dancer of the same name,
 famous here. Could she be the beauty
I recall? And even if she is,
 what made the power of that memory?
I watch the doorman's eyes for any sign
 of wonder flashing through revolving glass . . .
at last it comes, his wooden countenance
 is branded as she enters, blinding the space

and all heads turn to notice, then to stare.
One mystery gone: she wears the face I dreamed.
Yet this would be simple, as any miracle
is simple, only strange because it happens.
A saint stands in the flame yet will not burn,
the statue weeps, the water runs to wine;
simple things, the flame, the wine, the tears,
yielding a mythic beauty in ten years.

So much for the lesser mystery, the great one
hides within it like a Chinese box
as we turn to face each other on a couch
and twilight closes around the cornered hour.
What made the memory? Beauty alone
fades quickly in the mind and leaves no trace.
Was I like a silly goose awakening then
from a second birth, and imprinted upon

the first bright thing I saw, which was her face?
If so, it might have been most anyone.
She listens, reticent as I explain
my silence, that began so long ago.
She hears me, and eyes of beryl begin to glow
and glisten as I pause, begin again
in the dwindling hour that must contain ten years
or crack like crystal brimming with liquid fire,

and now reminds me she is the one who called
     though I am the one to blame for getting lost.
"And I have struggled with a coeval ghost
     or angel, in rooms of mirrors, stage after stage,
New York to Paris, ghost with eyes of living stone
     that monitored each arabesque and spin..."
whose fury for perfection would have thrown
     the body and spirit of a lesser woman.

And she has come to see these eyes of mine
     read in the faint lines of her hands and brow
that courage held her ten years in my mind
     as in the world. It was not her beauty alone.

HOMAGE TO MALLARMÉ

1. THE BARREL ORGAN

Since my Vivian left me
to fly to another star—
Orion was it, Altair,
or the pale emerald, Venus?
—I have loved being alone.

All day I sit alone, but
for the cat, and one poet
of the Latin decadence.
Since my woman has gone
I love the legends of autumn:

slow days of September,
autumn's prologue, the hour
the sun rests before it goes,
when rays copper the walls
and redden the windowpanes;

the slowly fading echoes
of the last hours of Rome,
those languid poems that come
before Barbarian cries
and stammering Christian prose.

I was deep in one of those
I love, whose patches of rouge
thrill me more than the rose
flesh of a budding girl, and
plunging an idle finger

into the cat's black fur
I heard outside my window
the melancholy singing
of a barrel organ. Under
the tree whose leaves in spring

seem dreary since Vivian
passed by for the last time,
I heard the sorrowful engine
that turns dreams to despair.
Then I heard it murmuring

some cheerful, vulgar reprise
that once made the back streets gay.
Yet the tune reached into my soul
and called the tears to my eyes
as no ballad has ever done.

I sipped at that song like wine
and would not go to the window
to send down my coin ringing
for fear I might see the organ
was not alone in its singing.

2. THE WATER LILIES

That flaming July I had gone
searching for water lilies and the friend of a friend's
estate. Gliding along the reflection
of a double landscape, rowing through both I ran aground on
this clump of reeds in midstream, my dawn voyage ending
in mystery
where the stream swelled to a fluvial thicket, and a pond
wrinkled though unconcerned
by the indecisions of its spring.

Closer inspection revealed this
green barrier in the current concealed a low arch
of a bridge that flowed into shrubbery,
enclosing lawns. I understood. This was the park of Madame
X, the unknown chatelaine I had come to call upon.
The nature of
a lady who would seek out a retreat so damply im-
penetrable must be
to my liking. Surely she had made

an inner mirror of crystal
shielded from the glaring indiscretion of her days
and when she appeared the silver willows,
leaf by leaf, would shimmer in the limpidity of her gaze.
Bent as if under a vast weight before the stranger
would come to speak
I smiled at my easy enthrallment to the feminine
possibility, that
I might be enchanted by anyone.

Then a sound, scarce audible, made
me wonder if that lady would divide my leisure, or
hope against hope, was it the stirring pool?
The footfall ceased. O subtle secret of steps that begin and fade
leading the mind here and there as they wish, aswirl in
petticoat lace
flowing as if to surround the will in a watermark
by which she makes her way
heel and toe under sweeping brocade!

Does she know why she paused? Is it
to keep these reeds and my mind's drowsiness between us
veiling lucidity, holding above
my head the very mystery that confounds me? "O lady,
to whatever ideal your features conform, I fear
their precision
would ruin my deepest pleasure in the rustling of your
arrival, a certain
charm defenseless against invasion."

Separated, we are one. I
mingle with her in strange intimacy, in this sublime
suspense afloat where my dreaming delays
this hesitant lady more than any number of suitors
could do. How many idle speeches would it require
to discover
so intuitive an agreement as I contrived in
order not to be heard?
Now my will rests on the scales of time . . .

O my dream, tell me what to do,
render in a glance that virgin space in solitude
as in memory of this place I pluck
one of those magic water lilies that suddenly rise up
enclosing with hollow whiteness a perfect absence
made of new dreams,
of the joy that will never be and my breath held in fear
of an apparition.
I leave with one, rowing in silence

slowly, so not to break the spell
in my flight by casting a ripple toward the shore
where anyone coming might discover
in foam or bubble a clear simile for the abduction
of my ideal flower. Yet if the lady comes, drawn by
apprehension
something strange has occurred, if the lady, that wild, proud or
thoughtful lady should come,
so much the worse for the ineffable

face I shall never know! I pushed
off and was skirting a bend in the stream homeward bound
bearing away my fictitious treasure
like some glorious swan's egg from which no flight will ever spring,
swollen with nothing more than that emptiness of pure
self, exquisite,
a lady pursues down paths of a tidal garden, pausing
now and then on the edge
of a spring to be crossed, or a sound.

3. OLD TIMES

Spiderwebs on the casement,
the wardrobe is ancient too,
fading curtains, peeling chairs,
nothing you own is new.

Didn't you wish, my sister,
with a glance at time vanishing,
my poems might set in meter
"the grace of some fading thing?"

New objects displease us
and scare us with their cries;
their need to be worn out
taxes our energies.

Come close that German almanac,
the days it proclaims are dead.
Lie down on the threadbare carpet,
calm child, pillow my head

on your knees in that faded gown
and I will talk on and on
of old clocks and cracked furniture
till the fields and streets are gone

under the cold of night.
Are your thoughts wandering?
On top of the casement
spiderwebs are shivering.

THE RIVALS

Happiness, in the fairy tale, comes hobbling
disguised as a hag. And the prince takes pity
on her, bringing her to bed, not knowing this

is happiness, thinking this is just a hag who
for some moral he values beyond comprehension
has made this trial of his magnanimity,

and no sooner does he embrace her than she
becomes an exquisite young maiden
with no past and no future apart from his.

So a man I thought my enemy came to haunt me,
featureless at first, in the dusk of dreams,
then turning slowly toward the daylight

until at last, in profile, I recognized
my old rival. He will have his revenge,
I thought, sending that face, more hideous

than anything of nature's cruel devising,
to flame up in a wall of sleepless rage
between me and all that I must see to do.

And my God, I thought, this is like love
who taught me her lesson years ago, though
she was beautiful and this is a death's head.

My enemy came to haunt me, tirelessly
until, desperate, I kissed him, kissed him
dead. Then he slept, long and beautifully.

THE TESTAMENT OF ISAAC LAKEDION

Here is a Man come to this City, if he may be called a Man, who pretends to have lived about these Sixteen Hundred Years. They call him the Wandering Jew. I tell thee Sage Sheik, if this Man's Pretences be true, he is so full of choice Memoirs, and has been Witness to so many grand Transactions for the Space of Sixteen Centuries of Years, That he may not unfitly be called, A Living Chronology, the Proto-Notary of the Christian Hegira, or Principal Recorder of that which they esteem the Last Epocha of the World's duration.

—*Letters Writ by a Turkish Spy*, 1686

April 22, 1984

Here in a circle of light your sleepless guest
parcels his means to pay for the night's rest.
This copper coin that might have brought me wine
or bread in Gaza when I was a boy,
bargains for an atom of your faith.
Heads: Jupiter; tails: the Pharaoh's sign,
an eagle clutching the brace of thunderbolts.
Legend claims the pouch I pluck it from
breeds a new coin when the last is gone
and so it costs me no more than these words.
But do not judge these gifts by what I own
or think I dream to match your kindnesses.
You climbed that skeleton of broken stairs
in Lloyd Street's ruined temple, to be alone,
and saw my breath rise ghostlike, leading to
this heap of rags and bones under the dome
where I chanted Kaddish for company
until I seemed to lie among the dead.
Pity conquered fear, you brought me home.

Here you bathed me, served up bread and wine
while your daughter stared at my long beard
and blushed at the sly wink of my sunken eye.
Your wife smiled as the boy hid in her dress.
We stayed up long after they went to bed,
talking of Truth and Justice in your study.

Yet I could not tell you what I would
for fear you would lose faith in me, or worse,
believe my words and never trust yourself.
So I spoke of the Parthenon before the gods
burned it behind them like a bridge.
I told of Nero's dining hall wainscoted
with pivoting ivory tiles that could transform
green mountains on the wall to a seastorm,
and flowers of gems, more true to life than life.
I wanted you to see Jerusalem
before the earthquake tore the marble veil:
how terrace upon terrace the temple rose,
with towers of gold, and colonnaded porches . . .

Then came your question floating on a whisper:
"Isaac, I am a strange Jew fallen
among kind Christians. First my mother
then my wife, now maybe my children too.
Tell me, Lakedion, who was the Christ?"
My heart, were it not cursed to run as long
as that sun pounding at the source of all,
had stopped then, but called me up the stair.
Climbing with the dead weight of that silence
composed of ancient grief and newborn fear
you might mistake my history for myth,
I longed to outrage the whole bookshelf
but did not answer. If I were a scholar
with Josephus and Plutarch at my side;
if I were a bold philosopher
with no wage but the Truth, no roof but sky,
poet or madman, I would have tried.

I have been all of these. Now I am nothing
but what I feared, a man who cannot die,
yet owns the power to unspeak himself
in one rhapsody of heedless eloquence—
as if a man of chalk should seize the cloth
and dust away his figure line by line.

Who was the Christ, who is Lakedion?
Finding the bed tenderly turned down
for one who has not slept in a star's age,
I ransacked the drawers for paper and pen,
the coward's weapon and the hero's toy.
The letter may bear what seems too strange for speech.

  ★ ★ ★ ★

By Caesar's temple where the market crept
upon apothecaries' laden carts
I spun through diagonals of light,
holding my jaw that rang with toothache,
haggling over a little mandragora.
The smile that shone before him in those days,
like a cracked lantern, I felt before I saw
the lanky deep-eyed youth whose face seemed
patched from odds and ends of ancient faces.
A long nose here, a leaping eyebrow there,
held together by the smile that said:
"Though a stranger to Alexandria, I
would pit your brave toothache against the worst,
and guess it will laugh outright at mandragora."

He shrugged the goathair cloak that students wore.
I said, "I was born here twenty years ago
but never have I heard such insolence,"
then I danced a bit as the tooth sang,
charging him to cite some authority.
Poured forth a catalogue of witnesses
from Baccheius to Philinus of Cos,
to make me lose all faith in mandragora.
The stranger picked out catmint and staghorn
then led me North along the Canobic Way
past the soma where Alexander lay
fresh in his honey-filled coffin of glass,
past tomb and temple, gardens and more tombs.
He said it must be easy to die here
where the living live among the dead.
And I gaped, for as if summoned by the thought,
two Mareotic mystics glided by
whose cosmic eyes intrigued my visitor
although I warned their cult was under ban.

This Jeshua Ben Joseph, Nazarene,
came from Jerusalem the long way round
via Babylonia and Thebes,
consulting Chaldee mage and Coptic priest
upon the marriage of the flesh and soul.
Now he would study healing and Greek thought
in this attic perched high in the Jewish Quarter.

He bid me stretch out on a mat of reeds
and pounded up a pomegranate rind
with poppy juice and smeared some on my gum
while he was fomenting the foul poultice.
This Jeshua Ben Joseph was renowned
for undoing Hillel's legendary patience,
by vaunting a preternatural memory
of scripture, and mocking the Sabbath law.
He told me: After hearing the schools debate
whether the wife might dress in head-bangle
or golden tiara shaped like Jerusalem,
whether the lame should go out on a crutch,
horse with chain or Libyan ass with bridle;
after yawning through days of such disputation,
he heard the masters litigate the roebuck.
"A sin," they all agreed, "to hunt the deer
on Sabbath. But suppose a stag leaps through
the doorway, might a good man slam it shut?"
Jeshua called from the gallery: "Rabbi,
if the house had no more room than yours
one would be foolish not to shut the doors;
that buck might be the leader of his herd,
and one deer in the house on Sabbath is plenty.
Rabbi, would Moses whittle such a pipe?
Is the world a ring for angels and demons
to fight for souls according to our rules?"

Said Hillel: "*Man* inflamed the jealousy
of angels the double-winged Sammael led,
and made those demons. Evil is man's burden.
But God gives us the law to learn and serve.
Study, Jeshua, and peace await thee."
Peace might wait, but Jeshua would not:
"You so clutter man's pathway with your law
he stumbles if he does not sit at home
like you, sifting husks for grains of truth
while naked children beg outside the door.
Study Goodness Itself a little while,
lift the latch, and feed and dress the poor!"
Now Hillel, famed for charity, cried out:
"Go! Seek the hour that is not night or day
and there, there you may study Goodness Itself."
So Jeshua had come down from Jerusalem.

I slept. When I awoke the pain was gone.
I hailed a miracle. He called it science,
mastery of the numbers and the will.
How might I pay him? He asked if I knew
the Jewish Greeks (he called them Greekish Jews)
who read the Pentateuch in the full glare
of Pagan wisdom. So he came to me
when he could steal away from Medicine,
to share my desk and scrolls in the Atheneum.

That was spring. By harvest, the man
had plucked up Plato by his roots
which proved to be the locks of Moses' hair.
Then, up leapt the Patriarch himself
from Genesis and Exodus to show
his words were manna to the Greeks, their words
bent rays refracted from the purest light.
We saw creation's God as architect
who bears in mind the blueprint of a town
before his thought takes on timber and stone.
Man in God's image summoned a man of dust
and a supercelestial constellation
gave to sun and stars their natural light,
while real trees sprung from His seedless forest.
The Psalmist sang our method, word for word:
"Thus spake the Lord, twofold was what I heard."
We did unfold the wrinkled Pentateuch
till it lay smooth and bright as the rolled silver
heralds use to flash from peak to peak.

Jeshua raised his eyes from Exodus.
"So, Isaac, Moses knows the world's a bubble,
which I mean to prove to Hillel by and by."
I asked him what that meant, and he replied:
"The laurel tree outside the Atheneum,
that giant, rooted south of the portico?
Look for it there next time you go by."

The sun behind him made me wink or doze,
next thing I knew was twilight, he was gone.
Sunup, I hurried to the Atheneum
and what! It seems the land had wheeled around.
The laurel tree whose limbs I knew by heart,
though every leaf and bird nest was in place,
had leapt from south to north of the portico,
leaving no speck of earth nor a spade's trace.
I fumed in the open green, so recently
filled with laurel in my memory.
I'd grown up in a world of brazen mages
who could speak doves and paint the air with ships;
I'd seen them raise the dead who'd gladly then
die once more to be brought round again
in Soter's name, or Kore's or Cybele's.
So when he strolled across the garden smiling
I said I had no eyes for miracles.
We were still Jews and enemies to sham,
for life is baffling enough a miracle
and magic grossly *contra naturam*.

"But Moses," said Jeshua, "did he not turn
his stick into a snake, the Nile to blood?"
"When Moses does those tricks it's literature,"
I said, "with you I fear it's truth itself,
your vivid thoughts trespassing on the world.
If you can do it so might anyone
and life would fan into a million visions
where not a tree or mountain would be safe."

He said this was his lesson, and a Jew
might work a miracle to teach the truth
though not for profit. Would I have him move
the laurel where it pleased my memory?
We laughed, and left it for philosophy,
where for a little while things might stand still.

There lay the arena of our second quarrel.
The sun led our way to the study room.
I said the sun was bright in the South room
which meant to me the room was full of light.
But Plato had crowned the heaven of our thoughts
with such a sun as beat by day and night,
which was God's image, though by no means God,
the hidden, sourceless fountain of everything.
Moses knew, who saw the burning bush.
We talked across a table sun-bleached white
and he said maybe God was in the room,
which meant to me Creation, like sunlight
that springs from the sun and yet is not the sun.
And so I said "Creation dwells among us."
We sat hushed, wondering by what art
the Unseen, dwelling inexorably apart,
had made the room and two of us talking there.
At last he whispered "words" which meant to me
words but what he really meant was reason,
the spin of thoughts in mind before you talk.
God thinks and a flower blooms like speech;
He thinks the law and Moses writes it down.

I thought of the voice behind the cherubim
above the golden cover of the Ark,
a Voice above the ladder in Jacob's dream,
thunder on Sinai, words flashed in the dark.
All our thinking led us to this pass:
the world is like nothing so much as speech
streaming daylight from an unknown Sun.
And our Creator's powers and his grace
speak in rare moments to godlike men.
"So, Isaac," he said, "God is in the room,
the son of man as he was meant to be,
His powers dressed in flesh and words and light."
I looked at the floor, the roof beams, then at him
and said: "I am not Moses, nor are you.
I'd sooner face the real sun in this room
than think you believe that to be true."
"Isaac," he said, "are you not a word of God?
And speaking now, could you not speak for Him?
Are we not, the two of us, a phrase
from the sentence passed upon our world,
uttered in perfect wisdom and boundless love?"
I told him he might be, but I was not.
Moses might be such a suppliant Word,
his thoughts divining the way of natural laws,
but Moses lived in a book.
                                    As for me
it had been enough to say grass grows,
there's good in man, and God is merciful.
That any breathing man might claim to be
the Word that speaks creation into being,
was madness, death-defying blasphemy.

★   ★   ★   ★

That winter Cholera made port in our town
and Jeshua left my study to heal the poor.
They kept him days in a slum until the fire
he'd quelled for so many, turned upon him.
I fed the oil lamp beside his bed
and sponged him as he raved, delirious,
of men who'd begged him to dash out their brains
while others pledged their souls to marble gods.
He'd seen a baby crying at the breast
of a girl whose moonwide eyes stared at the sun,
the ring fingers cut from both her hands.
He begged me check the ashes he had strewn
for prints of the cockfooted Shedim, a demon
he said would come before the Angel of Death.
No footprints but mine, as I bore the jars
of potion that ran through him as through a sack,
soaking the blankets that he rolled upon.
Three days it took the drug to calk his belly.
Then he rose, and ate a little bread.
I said I missed him at the Atheneum
for we had many a verse to riddle out
of Ezra, Malachi, and furious Nahum.
Yet even as he smiled I was afraid
he'd leapt somewhere I could not follow him.
And finally he whispered, "I know nothing,"
with a dull sadness, brother to despair.

By Mareotis Lake, men studied death,
were schooled in ancient Thracian mysteries
and lived ideas we scarcely dared to speak.
"Isaac, all our learning is a cipher
if we cannot teach a man to die.
Let us go now where they study death."
I told him life was text enough for me.
Besides, our law condemns their secrecy.
"They know something, Isaac. Look into their eyes.
They know something. What is it they know?"
I told him no one knew just what they knew
though rumors had been ripening for years.
Some returned, as true to their silence
as others who were never seen again,
said to be honored in sanctum sanctorum
as constant guardians of the mystery.
Darkness that terrified me drew him on.
Pomegranates flashed by the Southern Gate
their scarlet blooms against the pale fig trees—
no sooner was he hale than he was gone.

I do not want to know what he saw there.
Once in a low tavern when I was young
I heard a greybeard scream at the deaf air
his eyes had seen Zagreus divided,
that this was the hand that reached into his side
and held the live heart beating above his head.

He still felt it pulsing on his tongue
and blood he'd swallowed would not let him die.
Hands out of a shadow silenced him.
I do not want to learn what he learned there
or in Memphis, Antioch and Rome
thereafter, as he gained such mastery
it made the tricks and thoughts he played on me
look like a boy's strength against a man's.

★　　★　　★　　★

I did not see my friend for seven years.
I had gone up to Jerusalem,
my studies having won me at long last
preferment in the Coptic embassy
to the Court of Herod.
                                    I began to hear
wild rumors of this Jew in Capernaum.
Fearing neither God nor the Sanhedrin
he'd raised so many dead and dying men
he had to work more miracles to feed them
and spoke such truth the thunder stopped to listen.
So after the first riot in the Temple
when he was summoned to the magistrate
and scolded, I met him as he went out.
His face had come together, but the smile
was gone. Now he was sad and beautiful.
He kissed me. We walked by the pool of Siloam.

I asked him if he knew what he was doing
and he said he had come to proclaim Heaven.
I laughed, and then I wished that I were dead.
"Isaac, you have not seen how men suffer
for want of bread we broke in paradise
years ago in our sunlit world of thought.
I teach, I heal, but many cannot learn
and Heaven must shed mercy on everyone—"
"Teach on," I cried, "for there is nothing else.
Heal, but leave the miracles to God,
leave God to God and learn humility.
Each life is its own struggle to make a soul.
You cannot haul us back to paradise,
man, woman, cripple, saint and fool
without voiding the world of everything
but you, in one sunburst of godliness
to make yours the one battle against evil."

His answer came to me before his voice
and I wept for the certainty that he was mad
and doomed, and I turned from him as he said:
"I am His Word, Isaac, and they shall eat
of my body who can never touch my thought."

I turned away. He went back to Capernaum
while I, from a whispering aerie of the Court
heard plots to get him for treason and heresy.
They showed him the mason's withered hand,
dared him to heal it on the Sabbath day.

Jeshua sadly bid the man extend
the pallid claw, which then commenced to throb
and burst full as the flower of any hand.
My coded missives warned him against this.
I could not stop his feeding the four thousand
or healing leper, mute and lunatic
who babbled, howled and grimaced, limped to him.
By secret letter, courier and prayer
I told him to stay out of Jerusalem.
But he came, reining the wild colt over palms
and cloaks on the caravan road from Jericho,
weeping amid the chorus of hosannas.
I could not reach the temple for the crowds
jostling to hear him muzzle the Pharisees
who schemed to tangle him in a skein of words.
He fought with speech, they thought with clubs and swords.
I would have said: Get out of Jerusalem.
Those men you shame
are marking you for sacrifice to Caesar
while Herod yawns and Pilate quails
at Procula's dream and quits the judge's chair.
And most, who do not love you, will not care.

Three stars arose, three silver trumpets called
eager pilgrims to the Pascal Feast
while I ran through town from door to door,
wild-eyed Elijah seeking the hidden guest.
Though he was everywhere I could not find him.
So I prayed the hour would pass away
and passed mine in a pothouse with green wine.

Signum bibendi calicis. The cup
would not pass away, sweat mingled with blood
fell in heavy beads on the garden ground.
Thunder of horses, lightning of torch on stave,
ranks of the tribunes slammed and held him bound.
While I lay dreamless on the reeking board
a living nightmare rose and stalked the town.
They led him on a leash from Priest to King,
sped by whipthong laced with spike and bone,
Praetorium to Palace and back again
till the white robe Herod lent to make him clown
king shone royal purple from the stain
that rose from whipstrokes, dripped from his thorn crown.
While I lay in a tavern on the road
to Calvary they braced him with the cross.
I woke to prying light, a dull roar like
the savage surf of shouts a fighter hears
waking from the blow that deadened him.
Hiding my eyes I stumbled to the door.
Under the sun I saw the spreading crowd
drawn by a man bent double under his load
as if he were hauling them on a wide sled.
And such a roar quaked heaven's one-eyed skull,
boomed from their hearts and tongues, a heathen cry,
a chord I'd known only as separate notes,
as laughter, pity, rage, the mad sublime
diapason of humanity
sang at once on earth for the first time.

They sang for him. He hauled them along
the road to Calvary where I stood by
cursing the pride and rank stupidity
of the wisest man that I had ever known.
I wanted to hit him. I wanted to hide
but stood my ground under the tavern sign
where he stopped to rest and look me in the eye.
Thinking my voice lost in the general cry
I whispered, knowing his love, feeling his pain:
"You would not rest before. So now be gone."
But all the earth stood silent as he said:
"I'm going. You'll stay till I come again."

I thought he'd turned my trembling flesh to stone.
The crowd closed in behind him, they vanished
over the hill. I stood dead still, alone.
I did not move until his great heart burst
firing above the cross a second sun
that would not keep its zenith but bent down
burning to spirit all it breathed upon
and taking away the light that had been given.
I ran for the Temple. Did he not
once say that he had come to set
fire to the world? Would this bring Heaven?
What is the future but some prophet's will?
I ran as earthquakes opened grave and tomb
and heard the rending of the Temple Veil.

I thought I would die of fright. And forty years
later when the Temple melted down
as prophets of all nations had foretold
I thought I would die of grief, and I was old.
Counting my heartbeats in a pauper's room
with a fading view of Pharos and the sea,
the first time I became a boy again
I thought it was a trick of memory
at death's door, a brief reprieve of vision.
I looked for my father's house. It was gone
from the ruined street I'd paced as an old man
where now I walked in youth and was unknown.
I held my ancient heart in a boy's hand
and wandered from Alexandria to Rome,
Paris, London, a stranger to every land.
O you that have loved and lost, living to mourn
the passing of some longed-for loveliness,
stretch your grief upon some twenty lives
to know the anguish of my memories.
You that have known the high tide of suffering
and watched your child preceed you into death,
I have outlived my children's children's child
and known such loneliness I cannot bear
to look at any scene that I have loved
or bid a cherished face goodbye again.
O you that bloom and fade, bright butterfly
of summer, can't conceive my solitude.
Who was he to deny my right to die?

Was it for spite? No, no, he loved me
and maybe hoped I'd have the strength to live
as witness to the truth of history
and guard against mankind's oblivion.
He said I would stay here till he returns.

Well enough. I have learned to love the world.
It's not so difficult in this morning light
of April when pear blossoms jeweled in dew
spin from glossy branches to the grass.
It's not so difficult in your new house
where I am welcome, blessèd and can bless.
Living, I have learned to love the world
and with my vision of the consequence
I would as soon he would not come again.

When you read this letter I shall be gone.
Daylight fills the caverns of the moon
and I feel that green tingling that comes before
a new life! Whoever lived so long as I
without being born over and over again?
I'll cast off this rough and mottled skin,
my scribbled face, my cataract of whiskers
when the new moon winks her crescent eye.

I leave this coin, that might have bought me wine
or bread in Gaza when I was a boy,
to bargain for an atom of your faith.
Some say the leather pouch I pluck it from
breeds a new penny when the last is gone
and so it is mine forever, like my life:
the more I live the more I am forgiven,
my heart cannot be emptied, nor quite filled.
Do not judge my gift by what I own
or think I dare to match your kindnesses.
The coin is copper but the words are gold
as a rose some lover dreamed, and waking held.

THE AMERICAN WHITE PELICAN

Calmly afloat some distance from the shore, the pelican
has been taken for a sail,
its moist feathers glistening in sunlight.
A large flock flying is a seraphic sight, wings beating
in unison, apparently
without effort. After a few strokes they coast
in faultless arcs, often at miraculous height.

Honeycombed with air cells, they cannot plunge from the wing.
But the orange skin hanging
from its bill may be stretched in the service
of gluttony, driving the small fry into shallows
as they arrive with the new tide
to prey upon flies and gnats caught in the rise
and lower life swirled in the drift washing seaward,

the great fish schooled to shadow the small, eagerly
heedful of taking life in
order to sustain it. All seabirds know this
and the time of its coming. Now the white pelicans
that have been patient in a line
along the beach, steal into the surf, then
so not to fright lugworm or gudgeon, smoothly glide out.

Some distance from land they scud into line in stern accordance
            with the sinuosity
of the beach, facing shoreward awaiting
their leader's motive. Then all is commotion: the birds
            flailing the water with white wings,
throwing it at the sun, plunging their heads
in and out, and stitching the blue to a lace of foam,

advance in a boisterous phalanx filling their pouches
            as they go. When satisfied
with the catch, they wade and waddle into line
upon the shore again to rest, standing or sitting
            as best suits them, leisurely
swallowing the fish in their cheeks. Then they rise
in a flock, circling high in the air, for a long time.

The white pelican builds upon the ground, a nest of sticks
            and twigs upon sage or sedge,
a home with low walls of sand around to guard
the chalk-white eggs, whose surface is rough to the touch
            due to the shell's irregular
thickness. The idea that the pelican feeds its young
from a wound the bird has gashed in its own breast

has no place among the facts, though it endures.

FOR A CHILD FRIGHTENED BY LIGHTNING

First night in our summer house the sky is falling,
breaking away in wide panes that crash in the valley.
And I am watching from an upstairs window,
thinking that thought is next of kin to lightning

when it crosses my mind the boy in bed below
may wake in the arms of terror and a strange house
while I am spellbound by one pine stallion
rearing at a low cloud bridled by lightning.

Then a bedspring creaks and my son runs crying
through darkness streaked and stunned, where I catch him
at the stair in midflight, hold him still running
from the beast that fled the hills to rage inside him.

Now that my child's heart is a study in thunder,
how can I tell him it will not call his name?
Nothing will calm us now short of sunrise,
gathering flowers where the sky has fallen.

SILENCE

When at last you would not answer me
I listened like a spy at Heaven's door
and conjured up a dawning, soundless country
where thought became its own best orator;

where crickets sang no louder than the moon
and starlight made more music than light rain.
O echo of an echo, reverie,
thunder tiptoed down from the soft mountain

where I filled the air with love words once
and wrote in granite to outlive my age.
Now though I sweep the verses from this page,
the blank space cannot capture that silence.

THE NEW MUSIC

Word-weary, I dream of some Valhalla where
I hear a god proclaim the swans will sing
once more. I look down from ramparts ranging
above thunderheads, and glimpse an opal sphere
that glows, and swells until it cracks skywide
with a silver-winged cyclone of swans who sing
and sing, until the audience of gods there
staggers like wild ships keeling in a tide.

In sympathy, the humblest of the host
whispers in my ear: "That world is lost.
The swans have come to return our gift of song.
Cloud—drifts will unveil a new world soon."
And gazing down again, I see the larks
from their heaven joyfully descending.